21 Things to Avoid as a Newbie Non-Fiction Writer

C. Orville McLeish

Copyright © 2018. C. Orville McLeish

Published by:

DISCLAIMER

The contents of this book reflect the author's views acquired through his experience on the topic under discussion. The author or publisher disclaims any personal loss or liability caused by the utilization of any information presented herein. The author is not engaged in rendering any legal or professional advice. The services of a professional person are recommended if legal advice or assistance is needed.

No part of this book may be altered, copied, or distributed without prior written permission of the author or publisher. All product names, logos, and trademarks are the property of their respective owners, who have not necessarily endorsed, sponsored, or approved this publication.

ISBN-13: 978-1-949343-07-6 (paperback)
978-1-949343-08-3 (ebook)

Table of Contents

Introduction 5

Avoid # 1 7

Avoid # 2 7

Avoid # 3 8

Avoid # 4 9

Avoid # 5 10

Avoid # 6 12

Avoid # 7 13

Avoid # 8 14

Avoid # 9 14

Avoid # 10 15

Avoid # 11 17

Avoid # 12 18

Avoid # 13 19

Avoid # 14 20

Avoid # 15 20

Avoid # 16 21

Avoid # 17 22

Avoid # 18 23
Avoid # 19 24
Avoid # 20 25
Avoid # 21 26
Bonus Avoid for Religious Writers............................27
About the Author..29
Books by HCP Book Publishing.................................33

Introduction

With over fifteen years working as a ghostwriter and editor, I notice common mistakes new writers make that easily become an editor's nightmare.

Since the advent of the self-publishing platform, many authors, particularly new authors, are trying to *'do it themselves.'* So, they source all the necessary services that will move their manuscript from a first draft to a published book, and one of the key services required is an editor. Sadly, many new authors try to cut corners or seek out the cheapest route, which is not always the best option.

Editing is a process, and, for perfection, a manuscript will demand more than one editor and more than a few *run-throughs.* If your manuscript is in bad shape, then most of your investment will be required for editing. If you cut corners, the final product will not be as great as it can be. In fact, your readers may be appalled at what you have released on the global market, and you don't want that. You may not care very much about this initially, until the reviews start coming in. Many of your customers will not look past grammatical errors, even if the content is good.

I have made a list of some common things newbie writers should avoid, which should aid in a smooth and more accurate and cost-effective editing process. It's a process and it takes practice, so give yourself time to grasp these concepts as you grow as a writer.

Let's begin.

Avoid # 1

Avoid adding pictures or smiley faces to your manuscript. Also, never put "(Smile)" at the end of a sentence.

I have seen this done many times by new authors. There is a reason we never see this in a published book, because it will not get past the editor. Every moment you spend adding these to your manuscript will require time spent by your editor to remove them. It gives your manuscript an amateurish look, and it can be distracting for readers. It adds nothing to your content and should be avoided at all cost.

Avoid # 2

Avoid the Overuse of Bold and Italics.

When writing your book, there is a tendency or temptation to highlight words, phrases, and thoughts for your readers. This is unnecessary, as readers are capable of highlighting what stands out for them throughout your book. Your readers don't need you to tell them what to focus on, and every reader will have a different experience while reading your book, so it's best not to try to generalize by assumption what you want your readers to remember and take away from your book. You can use italics for dialogue and bold for titles and subtitles but avoid using them otherwise.

Avoid # 3

Avoid the Overuse of Commas.

The use of commas can be relative and will differ from editor to editor. No two editors follow the exact same comma rules all the time. Some editors prefer to use a comma after the word 'So,' and others prefer to remove the comma. It's really a matter of preference and is not incorrect either way.

You should allow your editor to make the final call on the placement of commas. I have seen writers who displace commas and add them back unnecessarily to their edited manuscript. On many occasions, when a client decides on placing commas, the editor will end up having to re-edit the entire document again. Your assignment, after a manuscript is edited, is to check the content, to ensure you have said all you wanted to say, but not to check punctuation, comma use, etc.

The purpose of a comma is to mark a slight break between different parts of a sentence. It is used to make the meaning of sentences clearer, by grouping and separating words, phrases, and clauses. Any other use of a comma is incorrect.

Avoid # 4

Avoid the Use of Ellipsis (the Three Dots).

The ellipsis is used to indicate the omission of words in the middle of a quoted sentence or the omission of sentences within a quoted paragraph. In creative writing, the ellipsis functions to indicate that the speaker has trailed off and left a sentence or thought unfinished.[1]

Aside from this usage, ellipsis or the three dots should not be used. I have seen authors end the last sentences in each paragraph with an ellipsis. Once your thought is complete, a full stop is sufficient. Unless it's a dramatic writing, your thoughts should all be complete thoughts. Try to avoid the habitually leaving sentences or thoughts unfinished.

---

1   http://www.getitwriteonline.com/archive/101805ellipses.htm

Avoid # 5

Avoid Writing Clichés.

What is a cliché? A cliché is a tired, stale phrase or idiom that, because of overuse, has lost its impact. What was once a fresh way of looking at something has become a weak prop for writing that feels unimaginative and dull. Clichés are what you write when you don't have the energy or inspiration to think of a new way to express an idea.[2]

Writer's Digest compiled this list of phrases to avoid:

- **Avoid it like the plague**
- **Dead as a doornail**
- **Take the tiger by the tail**
- **Low-hanging fruit**
- **If only walls could talk**
- **The pot calling the kettle black**
- **Think outside the box**
- **Thick as thieves**
- **But at the end of the day**
- **Plenty of fish in the sea**
- **Every dog has its day**
- **Like a kid in a candy store**[3]

---

2 https://prowritingaid.com/art/306/What-is-a-Clich%C3%A9--And-Why-Should-You-Avoid-Them.aspx

3 http://www.writersdigest.com/online-editor/12-cliches-all-writers-should-avoid

There are others I commonly see in non-fiction books, for example:

- **I say this to say that**
- **As a matter of fact**
- **The fact of the matter is**

I have also found the following common words are usually overused:

- **However**
- **Essentially**
- **Thus**
- **So**

These clichés can be used, but should be used sparingly. The overuse of clichés is distracting to readers, and many times they are not needed to make your point. Focus on writing your sentences directly without the added platitudes.

Avoid # 6

Avoid Modifiers.

Unnecessary modifiers should not be used. They usually get deleted during the editorial process. As an example, instead of "free gift," write "gift."

Also, avoid the following qualifiers and intensifiers: unique, quite, rather, pretty, really, very, kind of, actually, basically, practically, virtually. These words and phrases are not as necessary as they may sound when you are writing them. Often, if you delete these from the sentences, you will notice that the sentence is not affected and it reads better.

The normal Spell Check feature will usually underline these modifiers.

Avoid # 7

Avoid Inconsistent Use of Double & Single Quotations.

The goal of every manuscript is consistency. Dialogue can be placed between either double or single quotations, but this must be consistent throughout the manuscript. Don't alternate use.

Generally, use a double quotation for quotes and dialogue. If there is additional dialogue within the dialogue or a quote within a quote, then those should be put in single quotations. For example, "When I say 'immediately,' I mean sometime before August," said the manager. This could also be written like this, 'When I say "immediately," I mean some time before August,' said the manager. However you choose to use double and single quotations from the beginning should be the format used throughout.

Avoid # 8

Avoid Overusing the Exclamation Mark.

This is an issue I have noticed with new playwrights and book authors. The exclamation mark is used at the end of every other sentence. This is grammatically incorrect.

Exclamation marks are used to express excitement. This is not a common emotion when writing non-fiction books, and we use the exclamation mark in our attempt to decide how a reader should feel reading a specific sentence. We should not make such an assumption.

Excitement is a popular emotion in stage plays, but a full stop is more appropriate than an exclamation mark because of the nature of the writing.

Avoid # 9

Avoid Long Sentences.

Shorter sentences are key to quality writing. Long sentences tend to be too wordy and can confuse your readers. In general, write as concisely and specifically as you can. It is easy to read and easier to understand.

Long sentences affect the look of the final format of books and tend to be wordy. Try to use shorter sentences to convey your thoughts.

Avoid # 10

Avoid Using Passive Voice.

Editors consider this to be a major issue when editing a manuscript. They may change some of the more obvious passive statements into active sentences, but they will not change all of them. Most writers, especially new authors, tend to write in passive voice, and it will take some conscious effort, focus, and practice to break this habit. Don't burden yourself if you don't get this immediately, but it is a good practice to implement changes in small increments as you write more.

Here are just a few examples of active versus passive voice:

Harry ate six shrimp at dinner. ***(active)***
At dinner, six shrimp were eaten by Harry. ***(passive)***

Beautiful giraffes roam the savannah. ***(active)***
The savannah is roamed by beautiful giraffes. ***(passive)***

Sue changed the flat tire. ***(active)***
The flat tire was changed by Sue. ***(passive)***

We are going to watch a movie tonight. ***(active)***
A movie is going to be watched by us tonight. ***(passive)***.[4]

---

4   http://examples.yourdictionary.com/examples-of-active-and-passive-voice.html

Remember, grasping this takes practice. Your editor may comment on this, but this is one of those recommendations you can ignore. However, you should practice the habit of writing in the active voice.

Avoid # 11

Avoid Starting a Sentence with "This" "That" "And" "But" "Or" "Nor" "For" "So," "Yet."

This is another rule that can only be developed through practice. Even I have not fully broken out of this practice, so be encouraged; we are all on this journey together.

The use of "This" and "That" to begin a sentence references something mentioned *(hopefully)* in the previous sentence. Many times, readers may find themselves going back to the prior sentence to know what "this" and "that" is referring to, so sometimes using these pronouns to start a sentence can be a tedious task for the reader.

If you have the sentence, "This dog knows how to bark," we know what "This" is referring to. But if your sentence reads, "This is the reason I don't go to the movies anymore," the reader doesn't know what "This" is, unless they remember what was read prior, or they backtrack.

'This' and 'that' are relative pronouns. The words 'while' 'and' 'for' and 'but' are coordinating conjunctions, and they can be problematic when used at the beginning of a sentence. There are instances where the use of these words is acceptable, but generally, avoid using them to start a sentence. Chances are, they are not needed, and your sentence will read just fine even after deleting them.

Avoid # 12

Avoid Writing Excessively Long Paragraphs.

Each published page needs to be divided into two to three paragraphs at a minimum. It helps to give a reader a breather when they are reading your book. Long-winded paragraphs can be a turnoff, and it is likely that paragraphs that are too long are also too wordy. Remember, the key is to be concise and specific when writing.

If a paragraph is significantly longer than others, break it up.

Avoid # 13

Avoid Capitalizing for Emphasis.

I have seen this so often that it's safe to say it is the norm for new writers. They tend to capitalize words they want to draw emphasis to.

There are rules for using capitalization.

Use capitals for proper nouns. In other words, capitalize the names of *people, specific places, and things.* For example, we don't capitalize the word "bridge" unless it starts a sentence, but we must capitalize Flat Bridge because it is the name of a specific bridge.[5]

This is a common practice for Christian writers, and there may also be some confusion. It's tempting to capitalize church, faith, fear, etc., but the rules don't apply to these words. The Christian Writer's Manual of Style approves capitalizing "Bible" and "Scriptures" as these are considered to be proper names. Also, applying a capital letter to *"His" "Him" "He" "Me" "You,"* and *"Your"* when referring to God is generally accepted.

---

[5] https://www.scribendi.com/advice/capitalization.en.html

Avoid # 14

Avoid Inserting Page Breaks.

Unless you know what you are doing, avoid this. Page breaks are the responsibility of your interior book formatter, and when a newbie messes with page breaks, margins, and gutters, it can cause problems later. I have had to recreate a document from scratch because of this issue.

Your job as an author is to write. It is your editor's job to make your writing better/perfect, and it is the job of your interior book designer to format your book. You may think you are helping or saving yourself some money in the long haul, but you may end up causing unfixable errors in your manuscript.

Avoid # 15

Avoid Slang and Creole.

It's tempting to use slangs and creole, especially when you are from the Caribbean, but keep in mind that most people will not understand it. If you do feel like using it, do so sparingly, and please explain it for those who are not familiar with the terms or language.

Avoid # 16

Avoid Name Calling.

Be careful with this one. It's a controversial issue. The worst-case scenario is that you can be sued for defamation of character, but this is only if the one suing you can prove that you told a lie that affected their public reputation.

To publish the name of others in your book, especially those who may be connected to the story you are telling, you need their permission. It is advisable to get their permission in writing as well, as sensitive information shared about others in public can be damaging or cause offense.

Be careful how you write aspects of your story that directly affect others. One good practice is to change real names to fictitious names and tweak locations, etc. a bit so people can't easily identify who you are talking about. In this case, it is better to be safe than sorry.

Avoid # 17

Avoid Second-Guessing Yourself.

Write with Authority. No one is going to take you seriously unless you take yourself seriously. Stop second-guessing yourself and calling your own authority into question. The best way to do this is by removing statements from your writing that weaken your authority. Here are some examples:

- I think
- Maybe
- I believe
- In my opinion

Write with authority, and you will be seen as an authority.[6] Be confident in what you have to say because you are now speaking to a global audience. Anyone can pick up a copy of your book, and they want to see confidence radiating from the person speaking to them.

---

6   https://daringtolivefully.com/nonfiction-writing-tips

Avoid # 18

Avoid Fragmenting Your Story.

Telling a story in a fragmented style, or what is called 'nonlinear' storytelling, is one of my favorite kinds of writing. The problem is, you need to understand it and be able to do it well so your readers are not confused. It is better to tell your story in a linear fashion. Go from year to year, from incident to incident, and avoid jumping forward, then going backward, etc. until you are skilled in this area. In other words, don't get ahead of yourself.

You have seen movies that start at the end and then go back a few days and work its way back to where it started. That is acceptable. What you want to avoid is talking about your childhood, jumping to an incident when you were a teenager, then speak about your marriage and go back to your childhood.

Also, if you are going to share information, please at least give a summary of what you are talking about. For example, don't just say you are going to pick up your son when you have not previously mentioned that you had a child.

When writing biographies or memoirs, you don't have to share every detail, but what you do talk about should be satisfactorily explained, and it should flow, so it is easy to follow.

Avoid # 19

Avoid Switching Between First & Third Person.

This can be difficult to do if you are not an experienced writer, but if your manuscript has several points of view (POV), your editor is going to have a headache.

The idea here is to be consistent. You need to decide before you start writing the book what perspective you will write from. If it's first person, then be consistent throughout, and never, under no circumstance, should you switch to third person.

An example of first person is:

> "It was times like these when I thought my father, who hated guns and had never been to any wars, was the bravest man who ever lived." – *To Kill a Mockingbird* by Harper Lee

An example of third person is:

> "He drank an Anis at the bar and looked at the people. They were all waiting reasonably for the train. He went out through the bead curtain. She was sitting at the table and smiled at him." – Ernest Hemingway, *"Hills Like White Elephants"*

Avoid # 20

Avoid Fluff.

Don't write just to increase word count or to make your book bigger. I know you want to have so many pages, but if you don't have the content to fill it, don't do it.

Readers have an uncanny ability to identify *'fluff'* when they see it. It's like that music album we buy just to hear one song. How we wish all the other songs were as good as that one song.

The quality content in many books can be found in the last few chapters. That's what the author really wanted to write about but was told he should set a foundation. Often, the foundation is nothing but *'fluff'* to make one's book bigger.

Be focused when writing your book and only write what matters.

Avoid # 21

Avoid Plagiarizing.

Plagiarism is defined by the online dictionary as, *"the practice of taking someone else's work or ideas and passing them off as one's own."* This is a more expanded definition, *"an act or instance of using or closely imitating the language and thoughts of another author without authorization and the representation of that author's work as one's own, as by not crediting the original author."*[7]

Under no circumstances should you copy big blocks of text from any source on the internet and paste it into your document. You can quote a few sentences from other sources but give credit by applying a footnote or stating the source in your bibliography.

Be as original as you can with your content. Even rewriting someone's thought predominantly to make up your book is not recommended. If you are not an authority on what you are writing about, you probably should not be writing yet. Study, get familiar with your area of interest, but be original in your perception and delivery of the material. You don't need to write a book similar to one already written by merely stating

---

7   http://www.dictionary.com/browse/plagiarism

the same thing a different way. You write because you have a fresh perspective on the issue. Any chapter in your book that is just rephrased material should be deleted.

Bonus Avoid for Religious Writers

Avoid Using Multiple Translations of Scripture.

The only exception to this rule is that your book is a theological study; otherwise, there is no reason to use many different translations. Pick one or two and be consistent. Include a note on your copyright page regarding the Bible translations used in your manuscript.

About the Author

C. Orville McLeish is the CEO for HCP Book Publishing and HCP Ministries (offering ghostwriting, playwriting, and screenwriting services globally). Cleveland is a published author, ghostwriter, playwright, screenwriter, and publishing guru who has been assisting authors to write and publish their books for many years. He has the skills, expertise, and resources to turn anyone into a quality and professional published author. He writes and edits books, stage plays, and movie scripts in all genres, except homosexual and erotica.

Credits:

Ghostwriter:

Six Steps to Success, The Day I Died, How to Improve Your Marriage, Family Planning, The Painting, Internal Security, A Glorious Child, Train Up a Child, Legacy Series, God in the Marketplace, Pray or Become Prey.

Sermons to Book:

A Glorious Church, Sons of God Arise, By His Stripes You Are Healed, Faith Builders, Jesus Is Your Answer,

Jesus the Blood and the Cross, Jesus You're My Healer, The Holy Spirit, and Power.

Screenwriter:

The Rock, The Science of Religion, He Watches Over Me, The Waiting Room, The Potter's House, Detour, Chloe Cleopatra Taylor, A Christmas Wedding, Stuart Hamblem, The Whole Truth, Trans Siberia, Less Than Ideal, Little Flower Series, I Got You Babe, Monster, The Commentator's Retreat, Boat People.

Screenplay Adaptations:

Chloe Cleopatra Taylor, Beyond Time, Beyond Time: Journey Through Hell, King Coal, Endymion, Miracle Visitors, Journey on the Hard Side of Miracles, Glimpse, Pop 1280, The City & The City, White Jazz.

Playwright:

I Need to Know My Father, Christmas in Hell, Like a Thief in the Night, Christmas Family Reunion I & II, The Lord's Table, The Potter's House, The Waiting Room I & II, The Preacha & The Prostitute, Agents of Christ, The Mark, Forgiveness, Justice, A Mother's Worth, Agents of Christ, Amazing Love, Beggars, Bad Girls of the Bible, Celebrating Jesus, Chains, Christmas Light, Culture Shock, The Coming, Easter Carol, Expectancy, Great Women, Guilty As Charged, It Is

Finished, Jesus at the Sanhedrin, Jesus on Trial, Jesus; the Anointed One, Just Believe, Katrina, Love Dare, Maggie's Christmas, Mary & Joseph, Miracle Baby, Missing Piece, Rejected, Patterns in the Bloodline, Saving Nineveh, I Do, The Deliverer, The Exodus, The Room, The Trial I & II, The Word Became Flesh, Vanity, Who Stole Christmas.

Author:

Made in God's Image, You Have the Power to Create Your World, Come Up Higher, You Are Not Only Human, Overcoming Porn & Masturbation Addiction, Chloe, Beyond Time: Journey Through Hell, If You Love Me, Keep My Commandments, Interested in Working Online, Hard Talk: A Word for Today's Youth, Who Am I In Christ, God Wants to Be Your Father, Who Am I Really.

Editor & Publisher:

Goodbye Bugs Children's Book Series, Things You Need to Know About Non-Profits, Not the Only Ticket, 360 & More, Tomorrow We Will See What Was, Faith Builders, Baptism: What the Churches Have Missed, The Wonder of Trust, Evangelism Made Simple, The Restorative Kingdom, Knotted Strings, Beautiful Bows, Raising a New Generation of Believers, From Pain to Purpose, The Christian Counsellor, The Ignoramus, When Dreams Derail.

HCP Ministries and **HCP Book Publishing** are committed to taking care of all your writing, editorial, and publishing needs. We work closely with professional editors, graphic artists, and book layout designers to ensure quality and professionalism throughout the entire process.

Love This Resource Book?

I offer ghostwriting, editing, and self-publishing packages.

Connect with me:

Instagram:	@cleveland.mcleish
Facebook:	@hcpbookpublishing @ *authorcorvillemcleish*
Email:	info@hcpbookpublishing.com cleveland.mcleish@gmail.com
Website:	www.hcpbookpublishing.com www.madeingodsimage.blog

If you need any assistance writing and publishing the book God has placed on your heart, you can hire me as your ghostwriter and self-publishing coach.

Books by HCP Book Publishing

www.ingramcontent.com/pod-product-compliance
Lightning Source LLC
Chambersburg PA
CBHW021454080526
44588CB00009B/848